GEOGRAPHY *for fun*

People and Places

Pam Robson

Franklin Watts
London • Sydney

© Aladdin Books Ltd 2001

Produced by
Aladdin Books Ltd
28 Percy Street
London W1P 0LD

First published in Great Britain
in 2001 by
Franklin Watts
96 Leonard Street
London EC2A 4XD

ISBN 0–7496–4403–6

Editor: Kathy Gemmell

Designer: Simon Morse

Illustrator: Tony Kenyon

Picture researcher: Brian Hunter Smart

Printed in UAE

A CIP catalogue record for this book
is available from the British Library.

The author, Pam Robson, is an experienced teacher.
She has written and advised on many books for children
on geography and science subjects.

CONTENTS

INTRODUCTION

Geography is about people and places and all the changes that take place in the world. How the shape of the land changes over time. How people change their surroundings when they chop down forests and build roads and houses. How people manufacture goods using natural materials. Geography is about all these things. You will discover how people change the world, why these changes happen and what the consequences are for our planet.

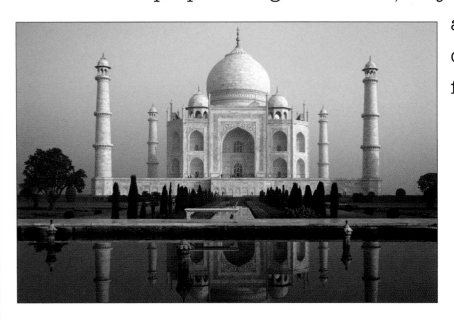

1 Look out for numbers like this. Each step for the projects inside the book has been numbered in this way. To draw the maps, make the games and complete the projects, make sure you follow the steps in the right order.

FEATURE BOXES
● Look out for the feature boxes on each double page. They either give more information about the project on the page, or they suggest other interesting activities for you to do.

HELPFUL HINTS

● Look out for Helpful Hints on some pages – they give you tips for doing the projects.

● Look at the Glossary at the back of this book to find out what important words mean.

● Always use up-to-date maps, atlases, websites and reference books.

WARNING

● This sign means that you must take care. Ask an adult to help you when you use a sharp cutting tool or electrical appliance. Always tell an adult where you are going and what you are doing when you collect information for the projects.

SETTLEMENTS

A settlement is a place where people live. It can be very small, with only a few houses, or as large as a city, where millions of people live. A city has lots of shops and offices and provides services, like hospitals and schools, for its people. A long time ago, people built settlements close to rivers, because they provided water and were the best way to transport goods. London grew up at a good location on the River Thames.

Street map

Continent map

A house is built by a river for water and easy transportation.

Roads are built and a town forms as more people settle.

The town expands into a city, with services, factories and many roads.

WHERE YOU LIVE

Make a 'nest' of four maps, each on a different scale, to show the first four lines of your address.

Paola Zaghini
14 Appian Way
Rome
Italy
Europe
The Northern Hemisphere
The World
The Galaxy
The U

1 Use a large-scale map to find the street you live on.

2 Find the location of your village, town or city in an atlas. Is there a river nearby? Now find your country. What shape is it? Does it have a coastline? Find the name of the continent in which you live.

Town location map

Country map

3 Now draw four maps, as shown. Make sure you put in natural features, like rivers. Glue the maps onto card and label them.

HELPFUL HINTS

● The scale on each map is different. A street map is large scale; a continent map is small scale. To get the scale right, trace from the atlas.
● Practise using scale by doing map 'nests' for places you hear about in the news.

TYPES OF SETTLEMENT
● The area around a settlement is its location. A village is a rural location, which means it is surrounded by countryside. A town or city is an urban location – a built-up area, with many buildings and services.

CITY
Large urban location. Services include shops, offices, factories, places of worship, schools, hospitals, museums, theatres, restaurants, post offices, galleries, roads and public transport.

TOWN
Smaller than a city, but with similar services (in big towns). Small towns often have one main shopping centre or street.

VILLAGE
Up to 2,000 people. Services may include shops, a post office, a school and public transport.

HAMLET
Fewer than 50 people. Few services.

FARM or HOMESTEAD
One family. No services except for electricity and telephone (in developed countries).

● Settlements built on the outskirts of cities are called suburbs. Suburbs sometimes stretch to join up with towns or villages nearby. These sprawling cities are called conurbations.

SHORT JOURNEYS

People make journeys every day. Each time you leave your house – to go to school, to a friend's house or to the shops – you are making a journey. There are different ways to travel a short distance – on foot or by bicycle, car, train or bus. It usually takes longer to walk, but it is good exercise. People drive to supermarkets to shop. Parents often drive their children to school. Many people commute (travel to work each day) by car, bus or train.

Brian
5 km
20 mins

Tony
3 km
15 mins

Lisa
4 km
20 mins

Tasmin
300 m
5 mins

Rashid
2 km
15 mins

JOURNEY TIMES

Carry out a survey with a group of friends to find out how you all travel to school. Present your information on a chart. You will need stiff card, scissors, paper, glue and coloured pencils.

1 First, write out a list of questions to ask. Do you travel to school by car, bus or train? Do you walk or cycle? How far from school do you live? How long does your journey take? Record all of your friends' answers on a sheet of paper.

2 Draw and cut out a strip of coloured card for each friend. Cut one end of each card strip into an arrow shape.

PEDESTRIANS

● People who walk along pavements and footpaths are called pedestrians. In Britain, some children walk to school in a 'walking bus'. Parents lead the 'bus' and collect children along the route.

● Children in some parts of the world have to walk many kilometres each day to get to school.

Anna
500 m
10 mins

Demi
1 km
10 mins

Alex
3 km
6 mins

3 Draw a symbol of your school in the centre of a large circle of card. Arrange the arrows around the school. Draw transport symbols, as shown here. Glue the correct symbol onto each arrow. Write labels on small pieces of card to show how far each person travels and how long it takes.

Car **Bus**

Bicycle **Walk**

4 Now rearrange the arrows to show how each person travels home from school. Do they use the same forms of transport as they used in the morning? Make new arrows, symbols or labels for any changes.

SERVICES CHART

● Redo the chart to show the services you visit from home, such as shops and the library. Put your home at the centre of the circle and arrange the arrows to show which form of transport you use to get to each service. Write labels to show distances and journey times.

LONG JOURNEYS

In earlier times, large numbers of people moved from one region to another, seeking better living conditions and opportunities. But travelling was hard, and people moved short distances. Today, we live in a global community, in which many people can travel long distances quickly and easily. The result is that people from many different countries now live in cities like New York or London, yet keep close contact with family members in their countries of origin.

A MOVING STORY

Make a 'family map' to show all the places that you and your family have links with. You need a large map of the world, a pencil, tracing paper, coloured wool, scissors and drawing pins.

Grandparents' generation (2 twists)

1 Do some research about your family tree. Ask questions and look in family albums. Where were you born? Where were your parents and grandparents born? If you have a stepfamily, include them in your research too.

2 Trace the part of the world map you need. It may be just one country if your family has always lived there. Colour it and label the continents, countries or towns. Mark your birthplace in pencil. Draw an arrow from there to the place you lived next, then to the place after that, and so on.

3 Cut lengths of wool. Choose a different colour for each generation of your family. Pin one end of your colour of wool to the place where you were born. Follow the arrows with the wool, pinning it at each new place.

**Parents'
generation
(1 twist)**

4 To show the 'life journey' taken by your parents and grandparents, twist different colours of wool around your first strand. Add a twist for each generation. Place and pin the twists as you did for your own life journey. Write labels to show the dates your family moved from place to place.

MIGRATION

● People move for many different reasons, both within their own country and to other countries. Some move to live near family members who have already migrated.

● Some families move from the countryside to large cities to look for work. Most people in developed countries now live in urban locations.

● Some people escape the pollution and litter of cities to live in the countryside. Sometimes, they commute (travel every day) to work in the city.

● People who are forced to leave their own country, because they are living in danger, are called refugees. They seek refuge (a place to feel safe) in other countries. There are many thousands of refugees in the world today. Some escape from war or cruelty and others flee from natural disasters, such as earthquakes or floods.

WORLD WEATHER

Climate – the usual pattern of weather in a place – affects the way people live. Climate depends mainly on latitude, which is how far north or south of the Equator a place is (see below). Countries in tropical latitudes, close to the Equator, have a hot, wet climate. Countries in temperate latitudes (between the tropics and the poles) have a mild climate. Altitude, which means height above sea level, also affects climate. Places at high altitudes are always cool, no matter where in the world they are.

LATITUDE AND LONGITUDE

● Numbered lines on maps and globes show latitude (horizontal lines) and longitude (vertical lines). Latitude is measured north or south of the Equator, the zero degree (0°) line of latitude. The tropics lie between 0° and 23°N and 23°S. Temperate regions lie between the tropics and 60°N and 60°S. Longitude is measured in degrees east or west of the prime meridian, which runs through London.

Prime meridian
60°N
Temperate region
23°N
Tropics
Equator, 0°

CHART IT

Make a chart to show the climate in cities in different parts of the world. You will need an atlas, tracing paper, pencils, a ruler, scissors and glue.

Aswan
24°N, 32°E
Aswan is in Egypt, on the banks of the River Nile. The climate is very hot and dry – it hardly ever rains there at all. July is the hottest month.

Bogota
4°N, 74°W

1 Look in the atlas index to find the country and continent in which each city is located. Trace country maps from the atlas and mark the location of each city you have chosen. Glue the maps onto your chart. Find the latitude and longitude for each city from the numbers on the atlas map grids.

Write labels about each place. Does it get a lot of rain? Which is the hottest month?

2 Find monthly temperature and rainfall averages from the atlas. Plot these onto graphs, then glue the graphs onto your chart. If you cannot find monthly rainfall, write in the average yearly rainfall.

Temperature °C
40
30
20
10
0
-10
-20

J F M A M J J A S O N D

Rainfall = virtually none

Bogota is in Colombia. It is very high, so it never gets very hot.

Temperature °C
30
20
10
0
-10
-20

500
400
300
200
100
0

Rainfall mms

J F M A M J J A S O N D

Manila is in the Philippines in Southeast Asia. It rains a lot and is hot most of the year. The climate is very humid.

Temperature °C
30
20
10
0
-10
-20

500
400
300
200
100
0

Rainfall mms

J F M A M J J A S O N D

Manila
14°N, 121°E

Latitude and longitude

SEASONS

● Places in temperate regions have four seasons a year. Seasons happen because the Earth tilts on its axis as it circles the Sun. As one hemisphere (half of the Earth) leans towards the Sun, it has summer, while the other half leans away, and has winter. The Earth takes a full year to circle the Sun. The Sun shines almost directly over the Equator all year, so it is always hot there.

Summer in the southern hemisphere

Winter in the northern hemisphere

Sun

Equator

Summer in the northern hemisphere

Winter in the southern hemisphere

● In tropical places, there are only two seasons each year, a wet season and a dry season. Floods often occur in the wet season. In rural parts of developing countries, this makes travel hard. Roads become muddy and are sometimes washed away.

13

HOMES

Climate and location – whether a place is urban or rural – determine what kinds of home people build. In places with a cold climate, houses often have basements and double-glazed windows. In hot countries, homes must provide shade from the Sun. In areas with high rainfall, roofs must be sloped to let water run off easily. Urban locations in every climate usually have blocks of flats, so that many people can live in a small area.

TEMPERATE CLIMATE HOMES
Brick, stone or wood, with big windows to let in light. Sloping roofs let rain run off easily.

Equator

COLD CLIMATE HOMES
Sloping, ridged roofs with an overhang to protect balconies and people below from sliding snow. Often wooden walls.

HOT, DRY CLIMATE HOMES
Often rectangular, with a flat roof. Small windows and thick walls keep out the Sun.

HOT, WET CLIMATE HOMES
Often wooden walls, raised on platforms to allow cool air to circulate. Roofs often made out of corrugated iron.

PLAY THE HOUSE GAME
Learn about climates and homes by making this card game for two players. You will need stiff card and coloured pencils.

Temperate climate set

Cold climate set

1 First, copy and cut out two of each card shown here, so that you have 32 cards altogether. Each set represents one climate. Three cards show house types and one is the matching climate card.

Hot, wet climate set

Hot, dry climate set

2 Deal four cards each. Lay the remaining cards face down in a pile. The first player picks up the top card then throws a card away. Lay the unwanted cards face up in a pile. The next player can pick up the top card from either pile. The winner is the first to collect one full set.

SHANTY TOWNS
● In developing countries, many very poor people live in shanty towns on the outskirts of large cities. Most have moved near the city to look for work. They live in makeshift homes built from cardboard, corrugated iron or plywood. The shanty towns have no running water or electricity.

POLLUTING THE STREETS

Pollution in the world's many busy cities can make them unpleasant, dirty places to live in. Air pollution is caused by burning fossil fuels in homes, factories and cars, which produces smoke and exhaust gases. Litter is also a form of pollution. Most litter that people leave behind in streets and parks is packaging, such as crisp packets or drink cartons. Some litter is dangerous – broken bottles can cut people, and plastic bags can suffocate animals or small children.

CLEAN SWEEP

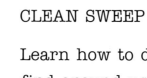

Learn how to dispose of the rubbish we find around us by making and playing the litter game. You will need stiff card, scissors, glue and coloured pencils.

1 Ask an adult to help you cut out a board from stiff card. Colour it to look like a local park.

2 Cut out 20 red cards. Draw on pictures of items of rubbish that you might find in a park.

3 Cut out 20 green cards. Leave 10 cards blank. Draw pictures of objects you would like to see in the park, such as flowers and benches, onto the other 10 cards. Cut out 20 smaller cards. Put a minus sign on 10 of them and a plus sign on the other 10. Mix them up and lay them face down in a pile.

4 Make a tray with four compartments, as shown below. Colour and label each one with a different way of dealing with rubbish.

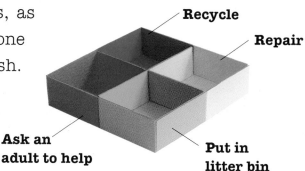

Recycle

Repair

Ask an adult to help

Put in litter bin

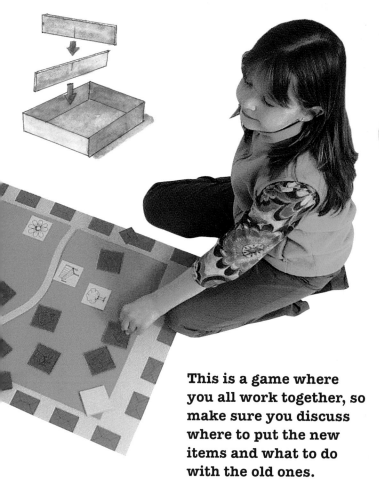

This is a game where you all work together, so make sure you discuss where to put the new items and what to do with the old ones.

5 The aim of the game is to work as a team to clear the park of rubbish. Place the 20 red litter cards over the board to look like litter on the ground. Take turns to pick a card from the plus or minus card pile. If you pick a minus card, remove a piece of litter. Discuss with the team what to do with it, then put it in the correct section in the tray. Can it be recycled? Should it be thrown in the litter bin? Is it dangerous? Should you ask an adult to help?

6 If you pick a plus card, select a green card. If it has a picture on it, discuss the best place to put it in the park. If it is blank, draw what you would like to see in the park, then position it. The game finishes when there is no litter left and the park has been 'landscaped'.

RECYCLING

● Waste paper, glass and aluminium cans can be recycled (processed to be used again). Glass bottles can be taken to local bottle banks. They are collected and then melted down and made into new bottles. The bottles should be sorted into colours first.

A CROWDED WORLD

As population increases and more people need homes, many parts of the world are becoming overcrowded. A quarter of the world's population now lives in cities and the cities are gradually spreading into sprawling conurbations. Some cities and countries are more crowded than others. France, for example, has the same population as Britain, but because France is bigger, it is less crowded. We say its population density is lower than Britain's Population density is the average number of people living on each square kilometre of land.

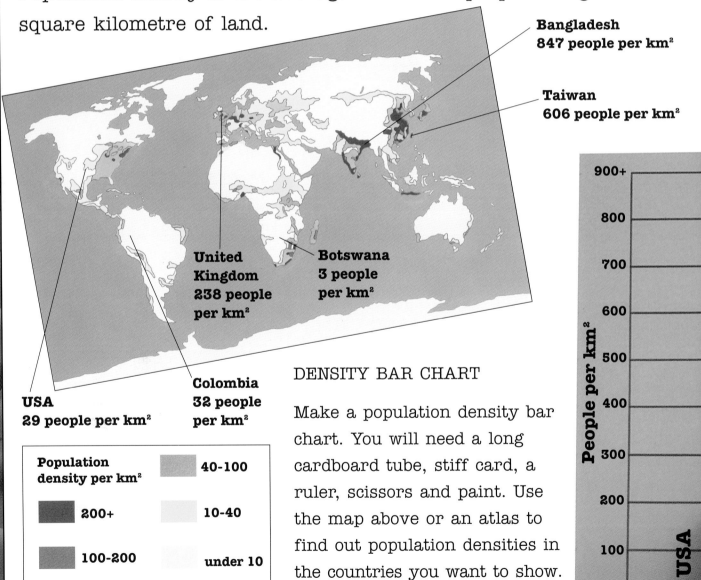

Bangladesh
847 people per km²

Taiwan
606 people per km²

United Kingdom 238 people per km²

Botswana 3 people per km²

USA 29 people per km²

Colombia 32 people per km²

Population density per km²

	40-100
200+	**10-40**
100-200	**under 10**

DENSITY BAR CHART

Make a population density bar chart. You will need a long cardboard tube, stiff card, a ruler, scissors and paint. Use the map above or an atlas to find out population densities in the countries you want to show.

People per km²

900+
800
700
600
500
400
300
200
100

USA

1 Choose a scale for your 'bars', such as 1 cm = 100 people. Measure and cut lengths of cardboard roll for each country. Paint and label each 'bar'.

2 Draw and label grid lines across the stiff card, starting about 20 cm from the bottom. Fold the bottom of the card to make a base. Glue the 'bars' in place.

Britain

Taiwan

Bangladesh

POPULATION GROWTH

● The population of the world has greatly increased over the last 50 years. In 1999, the United Nations declared that the world's six billionth baby had been born in Bosnia.

11 billion

6 billion

2.5 billion

1.2 billion

420 million

200 million

10 million

| 100,000 years ago | 2,000 years ago | 500 years ago | 1850 | 1950 | 2000 | 2050 (estimated) |

● As population has grown, people have cleared more and more of the world's forests. Some are cut down to harvest the wood, some to make room to grow crops and some to provide land for building houses and roads.

6,000 years ago **2,000 years ago** **Today**

Land Forest Forest Land

● Deforestation of slopes in El Salvador, Central America, caused mudslides during an earthquake in 2001. Homes built very close to the slopes were buried by the mud and many people died.

RAW MATERIALS

Everything we use and everything around us is made from material of some kind. Materials that are changed or treated to be made into something else are called raw materials. One important raw material is cotton. The cotton plants need to be picked, cleaned and processed before being made into fabric for clothes. Finished products, like cotton shirts, are called manufactured goods.

Iron ore

Limestone   **Coke**

Furnace

Iron

Iron ore is a mineral that is dug from the ground. It is heated in huge furnaces with coke and limestone. The iron separates as a very hot liquid and is poured into moulds, where it cools and hardens.

ANIMAL, VEGETABLE OR MINERAL?

Play this game to learn what different objects are made from. You will need small pictures of objects made from various materials, glue and stiff card.

1 Draw or cut out pictures of objects from magazines. Glue each picture onto card. Think about the raw materials used to make each one. A leather bag is made from animal hide (skin), so it is grouped as 'animal'. A book is made from wood pulp, so it is grouped as 'vegetable'. An iron railing is made from iron ore (see left), so it is classed as 'mineral'.

2 Write 'animal', 'vegetable' or 'mineral' on the back of each object card. Use these pictures (right) to help you. Anything made from a plant is vegetable. Now quiz your friends. Hold up each card and ask, "Animal, vegetable or mineral?" The player who gives the right answer keeps the card. The winner is the player with most cards.

String – vegetable (sisal or cotton)

Fork - mineral (metal)

Scarf – animal (wool)

Apple - vegetable (apple tree)

Glass – mineral (sand)

Cotton - vegetable (cotton plant)

Pencil – vegetable and mineral (wood and graphite)

Plastic spoon – mineral (oil)

Soap - animal or vegetable (animal or vegetable fat)

Leather shoes - animal (animal hide)

BRICKS

● Most bricks are made from clay and sand. These raw materials are ground together, then mixed with water and moulded into brick shapes. When the bricks have dried, they are fired in a very hot oven, called a kiln, to make them hard. The Ancient Romans used triangular bricks, but most modern bricks are rectangular.

● To build walls, the finished bricks are laid in layers and stuck together with a cement mixture called mortar.

JOBS AND RESOURCES

People need to work to earn money to pay for food, clothing and homes. A long time ago, most people worked on the land directly, as hunters or farmers. Then people began to work in manufacturing industries, using the Earth's natural resources – raw materials like wood – to turn into manufactured goods, such as paper. More people were then needed to work in shops, selling the manufactured goods. Today, few people work on the land in developed countries. Most work in city offices and shops, or in jobs working with people, such as teaching.

PAPER-MAKING

Paper-making uses up one of the Earth's valuable natural resources – trees. The trees are cut down and the wood is turned into pulp, which is made into paper. You can save paper, and trees, by recycling old newspapers to make your own cards and paper.

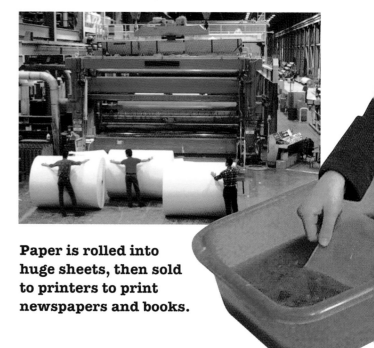

Paper is rolled into huge sheets, then sold to printers to print newspapers and books.

1 You will need old newspapers, wire mesh, a washing-up bowl, absorbent cloths, a blender, a bucket, thick paper (which you can keep and use again) and water. Tear the newspaper into pieces.

2 Put the pieces in a bucket and cover with water. Soak overnight. Ask an adult to put small amounts of the pulp into the blender and liquidise.

3 Decide on the size of your paper and ask an adult to cut the wire mesh to that size. Pour the liquidised pulp into the washing-up bowl and add water. Stir the mixture. Slide the wire mesh into the mixture.

HI-TECH INDUSTRIES
● All over the world, industry is changing rapidly. Many people in India, for example, now work in hi-tech industries, such as making computer parts. Many jobs that used to be done using pencil and paper, such as designing buildings, are now done on computers.

4 Lay a cloth flat on some thick paper. Lift the mesh out of the mixture and lay it on the cloth, pulp side down. Press down on the mesh, then lift it, leaving the layer of pulp on the cloth. Place another cloth, then more thick paper on top of the pulp and press. Repeat these layers, as shown.

Thick paper

Cloths

Thick paper

Cloths

Thick paper

Remember to keep all the thick paper to use again!

Add coloured paper or flowers to the pulp for decoration.

5 Lay some heavy books on top of the last sheet of thick paper. Leave for a few days, then remove the layers. Place your sheets of paper on newspaper to dry. Use your recycled paper to make cards or writing paper.

ENERGY

Most of the energy we use in factories, homes and cars is created from burning fossil fuels – oil, coal and natural gas. Fossil fuels cause air pollution when they burn. They give off a gas called carbon dioxide, which gradually builds up in the Earth's atmosphere. Fossil fuels are also non-renewable, which means they will not last forever. People are looking for other ways to make energy, from sources that will not run out, such as the wind, light from the Sun and running or falling water.

Burning fossil fuels in homes and factories, and in cars and planes, releases carbon dioxide gas.

Carbon dioxide gas builds up in the atmosphere.

Burning fossil fuels

Too much carbon dioxide in the atmosphere traps too much heat from the Sun. The Earth gets too warm, making ice melt and sea levels rise. This is called the greenhouse effect.

WIND POWER

Harness the power of the wind with a windmill. You will need thin paper, a length of dowelling, glass-headed pins, a small bead, scissors and a ruler.

1 Cut out a square from the paper. Mark the centre. Draw lines from each corner, almost to the centre, as shown here. Cut along the lines.

2 Fold each corner into the centre, as shown. Fix in place with a pin. Slide the bead onto the pin, behind the windmill.

3 Push the pin into the dowelling, with the bead between the windmill and the dowelling. Make sure the point of the pin does not stick out. Now stand in the wind and watch your windmill spin round as it captures the energy of the wind.

SOLAR POWER

● Solar energy comes directly from the Sun. Solar power stations (below) or solar panels attached to homes can capture energy from the Sun to provide heat and hot water. In hot deserts it is easy to trap the Sun's energy. It is more difficult in temperate countries, which have lots of cloud and rain.

Solar panels

WIND POWER

● Arrays (arrangements) of wind turbines are set up in exposed places. The blades can be up to 65 m across. The wind turns the turbine blades just as it spins your windmill. The turbines are connected to generators, which produce electricity. Wind energy is renewable and clean, but some people say the turbines spoil the scenery.

COUNTRY PROFILE – KENYA

A country is a specific area of land, defined by humans, that is controlled by a single government There are about 200 countries in the world.

Studying a country helps you see how different parts of geography fit together – how places and people affect each other. Kenya is a country in the continent of Africa. Its capital city is Nairobi. The zero degree (0°) line of latitude runs through Kenya, which means it is right on the Equator, the hottest part of the world.

Kenyans mostly speak Kiswahili, but English is also spoken.

Kenya is close to Uganda, Ethiopia and Tanzania.

North of the Equator, Kenya is hot and has very little rain. South of the Equator, there are 3 climatic regions: the humid coast, the temperate highlands and the tropical region of Lake Victoria.

Coffee, tea and sisal grow well in the tropical climate.

The rainy seasons are: October - December and April - June.

Mount Kenya is part of a chain of volcanic ridges.

PROJECT KENYA

Make a travel poster about Kenya and its people. You will need coloured pencils, an atlas and a large sheet of paper. First, look at a globe or an atlas to locate Africa.

1 Write a list of the things that you need to find out about the country. What kind of climate does Kenya have? Does it have seasons? Are there any mountains? How high are they? Is there a coastline? Use the atlas, go to the library or use the internet to find the information you need.

TOURISM

● Tourism is one of Kenya's biggest industries. Hundreds of thousands of people visit every year and tourist activities provide jobs for thousands of local people. Many people come to visit the beautiful coastline, but most come to go on safari in one of the country's many national parks, such as Amboseli and the Masai Mara Game Reserve. The national parks are home to wild animals, such as lions, zebras and elephants.

Kenyan national flag

The Kenyan flag is black, red and green, with a shield and crossed spears logo in the centre.

People eat *ugali*, a porridge made from cornmeal and water. They also eat *irio*, made from mashed corn, potatoes, beans and peas.

In cities, Kenyans live in modern houses or flats with plumbing and electricity. Farmhouses may be built from logs, branches and mud. In Nairobi, houses are built from bricks.

2 There are many different tribal groups in Kenya, but most people are Kikuyu. Do some research to find out more about the Kenyan people. What languages do they speak? What kinds of houses do they live in? What are the main industries? What crops are grown? What do people eat? On your large sheet of paper, draw pictures and write labels for all the things you have found out about Kenya and its people.

LANDMARKS

Tourists visit landmarks all over the world. Some are specially built by humans, as monuments to a great event or person. The Taj Mahal in India was built by Shah Jehan in the seventeenth century as a tomb for his wife. Others are historic buildings or structures – such as Tower Bridge in London – which are famous for their design or for something that happened there in the past. Many landmarks are natural wonders, like waterfalls or mountains. Postcards often show landmarks.

Uluru, or Ayer's Rock, Australia

Taj Mahal, Agra, India

Tower Bridge, London, England

WHERE AM I?

Learn about landmarks in this game. You will need small pictures of different landmarks, stiff card, scissors, glue and an atlas.

1 Collect postcards or cut out pictures from old magazines. Glue them onto pieces of stiff card.

2 Look in the atlas to find the location of every landmark. On the back of each card, write a few clues about the landmark, such as the capital of the country it is in.

3 Two or more players can play. One person is the tourist and holds up each picture in turn, asking "Where am I?". Players must guess the name of the country or city from the picture. Give clues if no-one gets it first go. Whoever gets the answer keeps the card. The winner is the player who collects the most cards.

CHANGING NAMES

● Names are like labels. But names on maps are often changed. Landmarks, streets, towns and sometimes whole countries are given new names. Zaire, a country in Africa, was renamed the Democratic Republic of Congo. Czechoslovakia, in Eastern Europe, was divided into two countries, the Czech Republic and Slovakia. The city of Constantinople is now Istanbul and Bombay is Mumbai.

● Settlements in different places often have the same name. There is a city called Birmingham in England and another one in Alabama, USA. There is a Boston, England and a Boston, Massachusetts, USA. Names can be clues to the past. Many people who migrated and settled in other countries named their new homes with familiar names from their home countries.

POPULATION FACTS AND FIGURES

The world's population, now just over 6 billion, is expected to reach approximately 11 billion by the year 2050.

Country populations

China – 1,200 million
India – 1,000 million
USA – 281 million
Indonesia – 209 million
Bangladesh – 127 million
Mexico – 97 million
France – 58.8 million
UK – 58.6 million
Colombia – 41.5 million
Kenya – 29.5 million
Australia – 18.7 million
Sweden – 8.9 million
Singapore – 3.5 million
Botswana – 1.5 million

Population density (people per sq km)

Singapore – 6,046
Bangladesh – 847
India – 291
UK – 238
France – 107
Indonesia – 105
Kenya – 57
Mexico – 49
Colombia – 32
USA – 29
China – 20
Sweden – 18
Botswana – 3
Australia – 2

People

● One in six people in the world today lives in poverty.

● Today, around 95 per cent of babies are born in developing countries, where food and water are often scarce.

● Developed countries consume the bulk of the world's food, fuel and water and cause the most environmental damage.

● The USA consumes one hundred times more energy than Bangladesh.

● It takes nature a million years to produce the amount of oil that the UK uses in one year.

● Denmark makes four per cent of its electricity from wind power.

GLOSSARY

Altitude
Height above sea level.

Climate
The average weather in a place over the year.

Conurbation
Towns and cities joined into one big urban area.

Deforestation
The clearing of forest.

Developed countries
Countries where there are lots of industries and most people have a good standard of living.

Developing countries
Countries where there are few industries and many people live in poverty.

Equator
An imaginary line around the centre of the Earth at zero degrees (0°) latitude.

Fossil fuels
Fuels like coal, oil and natural gas, formed from the remains of living things.

Generation
The period of about 20 years that separates parents and children.

Greenhouse effect
The trapping of too much heat inside the Earth's atmosphere, due to high levels of carbon dioxide caused by burning fossil fuels.

Hamlet
A small village.

Hi-tech industries
Modern, scientific industries, such as computer manufacturing.

Latitude
Distance in degrees north or south of the Equator. Lines of latitude are parallel to the Equator.

Longitude
Distance in degrees east or west of the prime meridian.

Mineral
Any non-living matter. Rocks and metals are made up of minerals.

Pedestrian
A person who walks in an urban area.

Population density
The average number of people living in each square kilometre.

Prime meridian
An imaginary line that circles the Earth north to south at 0° longitude.

Refugee
A person seeking shelter from danger by moving to another country.

Rural
Located in the country.

Settlement
A place where people live.

Shanty town
A poor area of a city, where homes are made from discarded materials.

Urban
Located in a town or city.

INDEX

PICTURE CREDITS

Abbreviations: t-top, m-middle, b-bottom, r-right, l-left, c-centre.
All photographs supplied by Select Pictures, except for:
4ml, 28 all, 30b – Digital Stock. 14ml, 14mr, 14bl – E&D Hosking/FLPA
-Images of Nature. 14c – Derek Hall/FLPA-Images of Nature. 15br –
Terry Whittaker/FLPA-Images of Nature. 22c – Philip Gould/CORBIS.